A Dog Can

LEVEL 2

/g/o/

DECODABLES BY jump!

Teaching Tips

Red Level 2

This book focuses on the phonemes **/g/o/**.

Before Reading

- Discuss the title. Ask readers what they think the book will be about.
- Sound out the words on page 3 together.

Read the Book

- Ask readers to use a finger to follow along with each word as it is read.
- Encourage readers to break down unfamiliar words into units of sound. Then, ask them to string the sounds together to create the words.
- Urge readers to point out when the focused phonics phonemes appear in the text.

After Reading

- Encourage children to reread the book independently or with a friend.
- Ask simple questions about the text to check for understanding. Have them find the pages that have the answers to your questions.

North American adaptations © 2024 Jump!
5357 Penn Avenue South
Minneapolis, MN 55419
www.jumplibrary.com

Library of Congress Cataloging-in-Publication Data is available at www.loc.gov or upon request from the publisher.

ISBN: 979-8-88996-780-4 (hardcover)
ISBN: 979-8-88996-781-1 (paperback)
ISBN: 979-8-88996-782-8 (ebook)

Photo Credits

Images are courtesy of Shutterstock.com. With thanks to Getty Images, Thinkstock Photo and iStockphoto. Cover – ESB Professional. 4–5 – C.L, Life In Pixels. 6–7 – Ekaterina, Faustova graycat. 8–9 – Makarova Viktoria, RavenaJuly. 10–11 – Bethlendi Tamas, Nata Bene. 15 – Shutterstock.

Can you find these words in the book?

dig

dog

get

hop

A dog can dig in the mud.

A dog can sit on a mat.

A dog can run in the mud.

A dog can lick.

A dog can hop up to get it.

A dog can get in a tub.

A dog can sit in the hot sun.

A dog can nap on a rug.

Can you say these sounds and draw them with your finger?

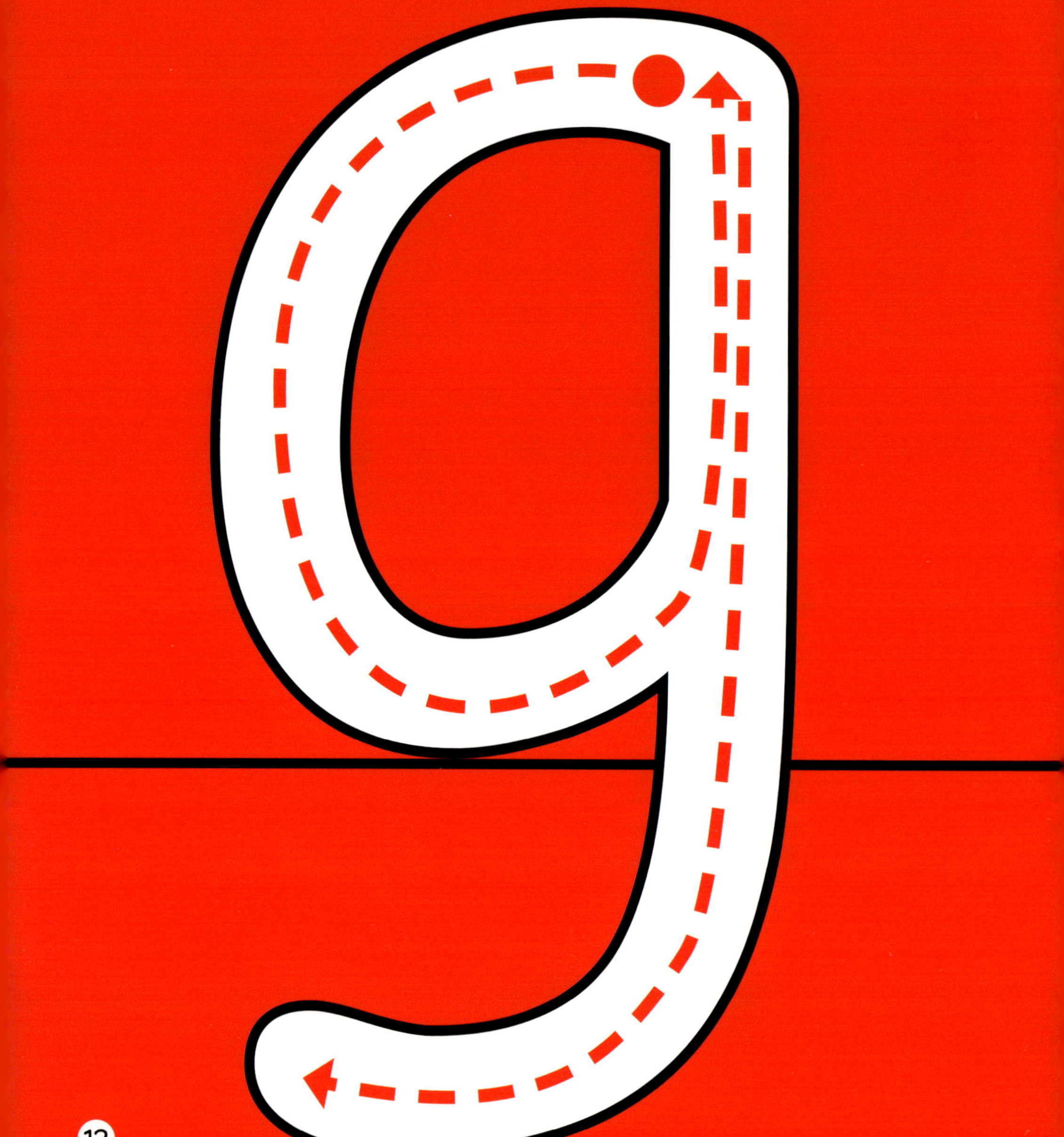

Using the Letter Bank, trace the missing letter into each word.

di__

__og

ge__

h__p

Letter Bank

d o g t

What other words do you know with the letters /g/ or /o/?

goat

gift

glow

Practice reading the book again:

A dog can dig in the mud.
A dog can sit on a mat.
A dog can run in the mud.
A dog can lick.
A dog can hop up to get it.
A dog can get in a tub.
A dog can sit in the hot sun.
A dog can nap on a rug.